Poems for the Funeral Celebrant

Poems for the Funeral Celebrant

Turning Tears of Grief Into Tears of Joy

RICHARD A. PHIPPS

Foreword by
Fred O. Berry, III

RESOURCE *Publications* · Eugene, Oregon

POEMS FOR THE FUNERAL CELEBRANT
Turning Tears of Grief Into Tears of Joy

Resource Publications
An Imprint of Wipf and Stock Publishers
199 W. 8th Ave., Suite 3
Eugene, OR 97401

www.wipfandstock.com

PAPERBACK ISBN: 978-1-5326-4766-6
HARDCOVER ISBN: 978-1-5326-4767-3
EBOOK ISBN: 978-1-5326-4768-0

Manufactured in the U.S.A.

*Dedicated to my wife, Kay, who is
always available for advice, encouragement
and participation in the preparations
of all my celebrant services.
It is a ministry we share!*

Contents

CONTENTS

Foreward

As a young teenager, it was no surprise that I began working in the family business. Following the footsteps of my great grandfather, my grandfather and my father, funeral service was a calling and the deep desire to help people was in my DNA. Now in my 36th year, I am humbled by the fact that thousands of Knoxville families have entrusted us to help them celebrate the life of their loved ones and bring comfort to them during some of the most difficult days of their lives. I have seen significant changes in our industry through the years, but the one constant is the significance of the grief process and how taking time to celebrate one's life with family and friends is a critical and meaningful part of that process.

In all my years in this profession, I have met few individuals that have as much love and passion to help families celebrate the life of their loved one as Richard Phipps. Rick is my brother in Christ and I consider it an honor and privilege to have Rick on our staff, and to support his ministry to families as a Celebrant.

Supporting Rick on a countless number of Celebrant Services as the Funeral Director, I am always amazed by his ability to bring a special kind of comfort to our families and, through thought provoking questions, allow family members the opportunity to reminisce and share memories about their loved one. With these memories he then crafts a unique and meaningful service that always brings laughter, thought, and tears. Rick's ability to write poems that bring out the special qualities of the loved one being celebrated is a God-given gift that, as a certified Celebrant myself, I would love to possess. I appreciate Rick's willingness to both share his poems and grant permission to use and edit them. As you read Rick's poems and suggestions, I know you will be blessed. My hope is that like Rick, you will have the opportunity to bring comfort to others. I also encourage you to take up Rick's offer to reach out to him for guidance and assistance.

Fred O. Berry, III
President
Berry Funeral Home
Knoxville, Tennessee

Dear Celebrant,

This collection of poetry I have written is for you! I have been a certified Celebrant for more than three years. I know the struggles behind finding that *attention-getting* start, as we begin structuring our message to family and friends of a lost loved one. Not only should it be a beginning that captures their thoughts and concentration, but it should also be one that lets them know right up front what the focus of your message will be! I use poetry!

My goal has always been to never conduct funeral services as a *dirge*, but as a true *celebration of life*, designed to feature all the contributions, positive examples, joy and love of the deceased! A message that clearly says, *"This is who your loved one was, and why his/her positive legacy is one to remember and emulate in your own lives!"*

In other words, I am committed, as a Celebrant, to *TURNING TEARS OF GRIEF INTO TEARS OF JOY!*

Celebrant services can be religious in nature, completely secular, or a blend of both. Whatever the spiritual focus of the service may be, that is between you and the family; however, the family's preference is *always* the direction you should go and honor, no matter what your personal beliefs may be!

I know many pastors, including those who work within the funeral industry, who adamantly disagree with celebrant funeral services that are void of any spiritual aspect at all. Their contention is *"If the service cannot be centered on God and Jesus Christ, I want no part of it!"* Pastors, you are preaching to the choir! When becoming a Celebrant, I too had to face such a dilemma!

I have been in the ministry for over forty years! Throughout my spiritual journey and study of the life of Christ, I am convinced of one *demonstrated* truth! Time and time again it is evident Jesus' life concentrated *NOT* on the religious, but on those who were suffering from rejection, loneliness, confusion, grief, hunger, disease, or mental issues! He knew these vital issues had to be addressed *first*, before He could ever capture their hearts and minds to receive and comprehend the loving hope secured in His Gospel.

In Chapter 19 of the Book of Luke, the religious were scorning Jesus for going to dinner with the hated tax collector, Zacchaeus. A pitiful man who was only searching for acceptance and forgiveness. The response by Jesus (v 10) to those complainers was classic: "*. . . the Son of Man came to seek and to save the lost.*" In Matthew, Chapter 20:28, Jesus essentially said the same thing, when He again addressed the religious crowd: "*The Son of Man did not come to be served, but to serve.*"

These two statements, along with all the relationship-building good things Jesus did for others, convince me that if Jesus were here today, and was confronted with the decision of choosing between a religious funeral service and a secular celebrant service, He would be the *first in line* for the latter! You see, a family may refuse to have any spiritual focus or mention of religion in their loved one's service, but there is one thing they cannot stop – *you planting The Seed of Christ's love deep within their hearts!* The Holy Spirit will take it from there! *We* do not lead people to Christ. *He* does, and many times through the *Seeds of love* we plant! As a minister, there is no greater service to a grieving family than that! In all my years, I have not found any ministry greater, or more fulfilling, than the honor and privilege of being a Celebrant!

The following pages contain a collection of poems I have written to *open* almost all of my celebrant services, but you can read a poem during *any point* of the service you feel appropriate. You will find poems that are for religious services, strictly secular services, and a combination of the two. You will find poems designed to highlight various characteristics, loves in life, vocations, ages, and precious memories of the deceased.

You have my permission to use any of these poems, or portions thereof, to help enhance the impact design of your own service. Every celebrant service is unique! So feel free to change words (including any names used) that will make the poem fit your needs! Allow the poems to even guide you in writing your own celebrant poem!

You can also contact me, personally, if you need help in writing your own poem, or to simply ask me to write a poem for you! Just email me at d.phipps1023@gmail.com, and I will be happy to offer my services in ensuring the tears of the family you are serving turn from *grief* to *joy*!

Meeting with the Family

YOUR INITIAL MEETING WITH the family of the deceased is crucial! It is the time you should be establishing a relationship of love and trust with every family member sitting around the table. They must see your empathy and compassion for them are genuine. At this gathering, which normally will last a couple of hours, you will collect the important information needed to construct the entire celebrant service! It is important to guide the family through this process. Below are questions I always ask, which not only help in developing the service message, but also any accompanying visual displays you may create and music selections to further accentuate the life celebration experience:

> "If you could describe your loved one in one or two words, what would they be?"

This is probably the most important question you will ask! The answer will often set the stage for your development of a theme!

> "What were your loved one's favorite hobbies?"

> "What was your loved one's favorite sport or sport figure?"

> "What were your loved one's favorite books/poems to read?"

The answer to this question gives you a great resource for quotes that apply to the life of the deceased.

> "What was your loved one's profession in life?"

> "Was your loved one religious or spiritual in nature?"

This, of course, will help you determine if there should be any religious/spiritual tones to the service, or to keep it strictly secular.

"What was your loved one's favorite music and singer/band?"

This question will help you determine songs to play during the visitation and service. You can even use quotes from a favorite song to enhance your comments. I did a service for a man who loved Patsy Cline. Normally, I would have played one of her songs during the service; however, it just so happens that my wife is a Patsy Cline impersonator! So, after explaining to everyone Patsy was his favorite singer, I set the stage for one of her songs. Instead of playing a downloaded song, my wife (complete in Patsy Cline attire) began strolling toward the front of the room singing *I Come a Walkin' After Midnight*, with a performance accompaniment track! Everyone there was blown away, and gave a resounding applause at the end of the song!

On another occasion, the deceased loved the movie *O Brother Where Art Thou*. This, by the way, set the theme for the entire service. My wife, dressed in a long white dress and singing acapella, came down the center aisle to begin the service with the song *Down to the River to Pray*. At the end of the service, everyone immediately went to her, raving over what she had done!

Of course, rarely do we have the advantage of impersonators. Don't let that stop you! Always be on the ready to think outside the box when it comes to music.

"What was your loved one's favorite color?"

Use this to determine what you and others involved in the service wear. You can also use color to set the mood in the room the service is being held.

"Did your loved one like to travel?"

"Did your loved one have any favorite movie, TV show or actor?"

This is another fun source of notable movie or TV quotes that can accentuate a life story or establish a service theme.

"Did your loved one have any favorite pets?"

"Did your loved one have a favorite food or dessert?"

The answer to this question can lead to many different options for you. We have given the immediate family gift certificates to their loved one's favorite restaurant. I have also used it many times to help decide on memory tokens at the end of the service.

> "Can you give me the precious memories and/or moments you have of your loved one?"

Stand by to write quickly when you ask this question!

Poems for the
Funeral Celebrant

Turning Tears of Grief Into Tears of Joy

MEL WAS A FAITHFUL member of a church I used to pastor. As the poem points out, he was a very short man! When it came to his service and dedication to others, however, he was a very *BIG* man!

A PORTRAIT OF MEL

A quiet, gentle man was he,
on that we could all agree.
His love and mercy kept us warm.
Truly, Christ's masterpiece of harmony.

O church, the Godly wisdom of this man,
our souls it would surely feed.
His servant's heart of sacrifice,
ensured our every need.

Although his stature was shorter than most,
five foot six in all,
a spiritual giant was he in life.
In that he stood eight feet tall.

The image of Christ should be our aim,
in him that goal was clear,
And now he lives his favorite promise,
"we shall be like Him, when He appears!"
(1 John 3:2)

I WROTE THE FOLLOWING four poems for the celebrant service honoring a wonderful mother of four adult women who dearly loved her. She taught and showed them many wonderful things in life, by sharing of her vast knowledge and experience, as well as through travel.

This was a service in which all four women wanted to personally share what "*Mother*" meant to them. So, I wrote and read each poem as a lead-in to what they shared with the audience. A beautiful way a Celebrant can work hand-in-hand with other service participants.

WITH ALL HER HEART

I know you struggle and question
as you suddenly begin to change.
It seems your world is falling apart,
but let Mom help, with all her heart!

Why suddenly are you looking at boys?
Why are you drawn to a world of noise?
It all seems strange and gives you a start.
But let Mom explain with all her heart!

What's this red spot on my face?
You ask the mirror as you look in disgrace?
Quick! Jump in the car and we'll head for a mart!
Just let Mom fix it with all her heart!

It's part of your years that we call teen!
Your hair isn't really gonna turn green!
Just enjoy and relax as I play my part.
Your Mom walks beside you with all her heart!

A ROAD TRIP OF LIFE

A road trip of life for eighty six years,
as she traveled fearless, filled with glee.
Though at times she possibly would shed a tear,
her spirit was always soaring and free.

She traveled oft' unhampered,
as she managed well her cares.
Any pain was always tempered,
as the wind blew through her hair.

Was she ever being reckless,
as the road would twist and wind?
It wasn't that she was feckless,
only curiosity driving her mind!

Yet as always the road doest end,
the trip can't last forever.
The Shadow of Death soon beckons,
as much as we hope it never!

But two truths remain about this dark creature.
Shadows ne'er can hurt you, tho' hard as they fight.
And their appearance is not a natural feature,
they can only be caused by light!

So as her trip quietly ceased and her
eyes closed silently in the night.
Startled curiosity was gently eased,
as she looked up and saw the Light.

HER HANDS

Her hands were always moving so busy,
their speed could certainly cause a tizzy.
Fingers like her own, oh so nimble.
I wonder? Did she ever lose a thimble?

In her hands, books read with eyes intense,
pages of romance and mystery suspense,
Thousands of words from which to learn.
Not a moment of prose did she ever spurn.

Hours and hours, hands in her garden.
Digging and planting til callouses hardened.
Geraniums, roses, magnolias, hydrangeas,
only few of the many she nurtured so gracious.

Yet hands ne'er too busy to care for me,
shaping and molding so truth I could see.
With her hands in mine knowing life can be cruel,
she lovingly guided me back to school.

Hands that created beaded ornaments of splendor,
decorated my life with love so tender.
How can I tell you of a life wrapped with lace?
How can I describe such hands filled with grace?

SITTING ALONG THE COAST IN YACHATS, OREGON

Sitting along the coast in Yachats, Oregon,
the wind coolly blowing across our face.
The red sun now tickles the level horizon,
as we search for sprays of power and grace.

They're migrating northward you know,
these massive mammals with calves.
Swimming to rich waters of Juneau,
filled with abundant red krill in mass.

Oh there! Can you see out ahead?
Black humps rolling softly with slapping tails!
What grandeur, how splendid!
These wonderful, glorious whales!

Then upon darkness we look toward the sky.
Another nature splendor is about to begin!
Suddenly darting streams of light so high,
'tis meteors sweeping o'er and o'er again!

No church nor chapel can display it more,
God's amazing creation phenomenon,
than when sitting above the craggy shore,
which is along the coast in Yachats, Oregon!

THIS POEM WAS FOR a woman who truly loved life. She was talented in many things, except the one she longed for the most—she always wanted to learn to *dance*! Yet, even though she could never learn this skill, that didn't stop her! The tremendous love she had for her family was portrayed in many other ways.

I WISH I COULD DANCE

My heart is filled with all the colors of joy delight.
Hues softly painted by my Lord's precious hands.
How can I release what is bursting inside?
I wish I could show you, I wish I could dance!

David danced before the Lord with all of his might.
In worship He twirled and he leaped with intense.
For God had clothed him with joy, as He did me inside!
I wish I could show you, I wish I could dance!

John the Baptist leaped inside his mother's womb,
when Mary, bearing Jesus, came to visit by chance.
I too want to leap, when I feel His presence in the room.
I wish I could show you, I wish I could dance.

How then can I show you a heart filled with bliss,
with two left feet, how can I display this joy from above?
With a hug, a smile, acts of kindness, or gentle kiss,
I'll glide you 'cross life's ballroom with His love!

OBVIOUSLY, I WROTE THIS next poem for a Certified Public Accountant. The family concentrated on how he used his gift of numbers as a true ministry to others. By doing so, he was able to relieve people's burdens, so they were able to enjoy the better things of life.

NUMBERS

Numbers are boring I've heard people say.
Who can fidget with digits the live-long day?
Who can add and subtract 'til the cows come home?
Who can multiply figures with the mind alone?

How can one help but from falling asleep,
Manipulating integers on a boring sheet?
Debits and credits, are the latter the more?
Writing and typing 'til the fingers are sore?

What kind of ministry could come from math?
To most it may seem a form of God's wrath!
Takes a special person to see the revelation,
of numbers' importance in all of creation!

Six days, all things made, not five not four!
Twelve disciples of Christ, no less, no more!
Are numbers important to the Creator of men?
Did He not write an Old Testament book about them?

He always understood his purpose so grand.
Helping those number-crippled to easily understand.
He wisely and tirelessly worked his gift from above,
To ease their anguish through the grace of God's love!

Now TALK ABOUT A fun poem to write! This poem was for a guy who loved animals, Mexican food, and to make everyone around him laugh! He was truly a joy to have as a father, a brother and a friend! By the way, he always pronounced the "L's" in *tortilla* and *casadilla* like "L's"!

LET ME TALK ABOUT A FELLA

Let me talk about a fella,
Who anyone'll tell ya,
In the rainy times of life
was your best umbrella!

He could share a sarsaparilla
with a stranger or gorilla
'cause his love for man and creatures
was simply incredibella!!

He never lived in Amarilla,
nor pet an ugly armadillo.
But he could fix a mean tortilla,
or a very spicey casadilla!

So often think of him for reala;
a friend that never failed to thrill ya,
with humor that tickled your bella

So as ya lay your head upon your pilla,
think with what he oft did fill ya!
The gift of joy . . . Oh my . . . he was phenomenilla!!

How many services have you led for those who loved gardening? Certainly this would depend on what part of the country in which you live, but in Tennessee, we have many! The next two poems seem to be the same poem, but note one is for a man who was married and had children, while the other was for a man who was married with no children. I've used these poems many times.

HIS GARDEN, HIS PASSION

His garden, his passion, he yearned for the Spring!
Alas! Time to plant, he and his birds did sing!
Slowly he tilled and prepared all the soil,
making rows proper depth, so the seed would not spoil.

Everyday to his passion he slowly did stroll,
to see if new sprouts had begun to unfold!
Soon they appeared, and with a smile on his face,
he silently thanked the Lord for His grace.

Weeding and hoeing, 'twas not work at all,
only pampering his passion 'til finally came Fall.
Potatoes, tomatoes, cucumbers, corn;
only a few of what filled his plentiful horn.

Much could be learned as he tended his passion,
one could clearly see the heart God had fashioned.
For deep within it God's love was secure,
and while growing a family he showed it for sure!

Each day to his passion he strolled home tired and sore,
seeking the sprouts of joy he adored.
As he saw each one bearing supper, smiles and lace,
he silently thanked the Lord for His grace.

Feeding and bestowing his love for them all,
he pampered his passion 'til winter's call.
When he quietly left garden, children and wife,
and met the Source of his passion—the Tree of Life!

HIS GARDEN, HIS PASSION

His garden, his passion, he yearned for the Spring!
Alas! Time to plant, he and his birds did sing!
Slowly he tilled and prepared all the soil,
making rows proper depth, so the seed would not spoil.

Everyday to his passion he slowly did stroll,
to see if new sprouts had begun to unfold!
Soon they appeared, and with a smile on his face,
he silently thanked the Lord for His grace.

Weeding and hoeing, 'twas not work at all,
only pampering his passion 'til finally came Fall.
Potatoes, tomatoes, cucumbers, corn;
only a few of what filled his plentiful horn.

Much could be learned as he tended his passion,
one could clearly see the heart God had fashioned.
For deep within it God's love was secure,
and while growing a marriage he showed it for sure!

Each day to his passion he strolled home tired and sore,
seeking the sprouts of the joy he adored.
As he saw her bearing supper, smiles and lace,
he silently thanked the Lord for His grace.

Feeding and bestowing his love for her and all,
he pampered his passion 'til winter's call.
When he quietly left garden, neighbors and wife,
and met the Source of his passion—the Tree of Life!

I WROTE THIS POEM for a lady who was, according to her family, quiet and reserved! Being a woman of few words, however, she didn't *need* to communicate orally. She had the unique skill of communicating with her eyes! A mode that can often speak louder, and more powerfully than any other venue in expressing one's opinion and thoughts!

WITH HER EYES

Silence was often deafening,
as she pondered what true or false.
Her mind whirling with wisdom,
weighing evidence of the actual cause.

With lips calmly closed and secure,
her gaze was void of disguise.
Ne'er a word was ever necessary,
for she often spoke with her eyes

Notes and lyrics consumed her,
as they developed within her heart.
Creation flowed unhampered,
through a pen of melodious art.

Passion for the gift of music,
given to a world in demise,
Was not only put on paper,
for she often sang with her eyes.

Affection is often shallow
when it is only vocalized.
The feelings that swelled within her,
words could never fully describe.

Nay! Nurture is surely meaningless
when stoic expression abides.
One could feel the grace within her,
for she often loved with her eyes.

UNFORTUNATELY, WE ALL HAVE to deal with death caused by alcoholism and drug addiction. This is a problem that seems to be growing exponentially every day! The following poem relates to these issues, one which I wrote in light of the family's request. His mother specifically wanted me to warn those who attended the service of the dangers they face if they were also battling addiction. She wanted me to plead with them, without hesitation, to get professional help. I, therefore, honored her request through poetry and presented it to close out the service.

I TRIED MY BEST

Do you understand? I truly loved you all.
I tried my best to show it, even through the fall.
Perfection is a quest no man has taken hold,
For all do battle demons, determined to grip the soul!

Day by day they hit you, slowly taking control.
Often dressed in beauty, to hide their ugly role!
I tried my best in this war, seeking for ways to win!
But victory is a personal choice, the will must start within.

I tried my best, yet you grieve because I lost the fight.
Perhaps you also battle addicting demons of the night.
If you do, my plea to those, relying solely on self,
The way to win is admit your limits and give yourself to help.
The way to win is admit your limits and give yourself to help!

THEN THERE ARE THE guys who always seemed to have it together! Those guys who had the answer for everything in life! Such was this full-of-life man portrayed in this next poem. He could be quite stubborn at times, but in a funny way. Thus, the nickname he proudly earned!

THEY CALL ME THE MULE

Opinions! There are many floating 'round and 'round,
'bout the world, its politics, and its people there bound.
But when it comes down to who's opinion doest rule,
I assure it's mine, for they call me the Mule!

You know I love you all, though I admit with stubborn wit.
You'll have to excuse me, if I cause you a fit.
But when I'm right, I feel obliged to take you to school.
To teach you the truth, for they call me the Mule!

Try as you may, to defend your hopeless views.
Give it your best shot, while your argument ensues!
I love it when you struggle with every intellectual tool!
But rest assured you'll lose, for they call me the Mule!

You will find this next poem a tribute to a truly generous individual. A religious man who was an avid hunter, fisherman, and skilled handyman. He was always devoted to using these qualities in his life to generously help others, *without compensation.*

A MAN OF GENEROSITY

I know it's not normal to think of others before self.
It's natural to serve number one, and leave the rest
on the shelf!
But the love in my heart refused reciprocity,
which is why I was called a man of generosity!

Whether fishing or hunting, tackle or guns are all you need!
You'd never go hungry, for all the food was on me!
I even prepared it, even if hanging from a tree,
which is why I was called a man of generosity!

I improved your home with new shingles or siding.
I wouldn't stop 'til perfect, no mistakes were hiding.
Doing it right meant spending time void of velocity,
which is why I was called a man of generosity!

I know it's not normal to think of others before self.
Yet 'twas the Lord who proved that love is true wealth!
If He could willingly give His life to set all men free,
I would follow His lead to be a man of generosity!

OCCASIONALLY, YOU GET THE chance to serve the family of multi-talented loved ones, who was good with their hands. In this case, you will discover in the next poem a lovely woman who was extremely gifted with refined abilities to garden and knit! She was also a loving wife, faithfully married to her husband for over sixty years, and a loving mother to her children. All of whom loved her dearly. He name was Mary, but you can put any name in the last stanza.

TENDERLY, LOVINGLY

Tenderly, lovingly she wove with her hands,
delicate yarn into masterpiece grands!
Colorful arrays of afghans so bright,
to warm those she loved on a bitter cold night!

Tenderly, lovingly she'd plant with her hands,
delicate flowers into masterpiece grands!
Colorful arrays of petals aglow,
to display God's beauty for all to know.

Tenderly, lovingly she worked with her hands,
delicate offspring into masterpiece grands!
Colorful arrays of personalities fair,
giving her all to their health and welfare.

Tenderly, lovingly she nurtured with her hands,
delicate care for her mate so grand!
Colorful arrays of a love three score years,
proving her devotion, even through tears.

Tenderly, lovingly He took with His hands,
delicate Mary, His masterpiece grand!
Colorful arrays of His love filled the night,
revealing the Way with the glory of His light!

WITHOUT QUESTION, I DO not need to provide a leading explanation for the next poem! This exciting woman also loved life! She was very outspoken, yet always took a neutral position on any disagreements that might come her way, ever claiming *"I am Switzerland!"* When I met with her children to begin developing her service, we spent hours laughing about this, as well as her talents of being a terrible cook and terrible gardener! Though, when not obsessively shopping, she loved the solitude of sitting on a beach and reading her romance books! She was a fun lady, whom all adored!

I AM SWITZERLAND

So I sing to bananas, is there a problem you see?
Life is too short for gloomy personality!
Carefree and crazy, ne'er serious at hand.
Yet silence from me if you don't understand.
For I am neutral . . . I am Switzerland.

I offer no cuisine that could give you thrills.
I serve crispy meat from flaming barbeque grills!
Ground chuck and ketchup, a meatloaf so grand.
Yet silence from me if you find it so bland.
For I am neutral . . . I am Switzerland!

Gardening I love, wild onions my herbs.
Flowers deemed ugly oft cause you disturb.
Invading beavers, not groundhogs, I take my stand.
Yet silence from me if you can't comprehend.
For I am neutral . . . I am Switzerland!

Fights ensue with mighty squirt guns you bring.
Alas, ne'er a match against the water hose I swing!
Sometimes it looks as though you're getting upper hand.
Yet silence from me as I cease to defend.
For I am neutral . . . I am Switzerland!

Okay, I like to shop, and do so 'til I drop.
Home improvement stores or shopping networks, will I ever stop?
Only the best junk I buy o'er and o'er again.
Yet silence from me, as you question my trend.
For I am neutral . . . I am Switzerland

I may bee-bop along as through life I dance,
sipping wine on a beach, consuming books of romance.
Aimless strolling along, curled toes in the sand.
Yet silence from me when the joy must end.
For I am neutral . . . I am Switzerland.

THIS NEXT POEM WAS dedicated to the quid essential *"Southern Belle"*! Truly a woman of charm, grace, and beauty both inside and out, who was a phenomenal cook filled with love!

A RECIPE OF GRACE

A little dab of hugs, with just a pinch of kisses,
a sprinkle of sweetness all stirred in love.
Baked with understanding, all basted with forgiveness,
a recipe of Grace from the Father above!

Can you smell the sweet aroma filling the air,
flowing through the senses like the softness of a dove.
The delicate taste is truly void of compare,
a recipe of Grace from the Father above!

The table is always full, a mere snack is not for real.
The burners must be full with skillets on the stove.
Truly it's a sin if it's not a full-course meal.
For they are recipes of Grace from the Father above.

The toil of the effort, in her mercy kitchen space
often soiled her worn apron made of faith thereof.
But she never quit 'til she finished her race,
making recipes of Grace from the Father above!

ONE OF THE QUESTIONS I always ask a family in preparation for a celebrant service, regards the hobbies of their loved one. In this case, the children quickly told me their father loved to take drives by himself, so he could think! Therefore, this poem centers on one of those imagined drives. The verses describe his thoughts about his wife, Melody (who he nicknamed *"Lil' Rabbit"*), as well as his loving instructions for his beloved sons! Note, this man was also a decorated Vietnam War hero, earning the Bronze Star with "V" (valor), and a Purple Heart for gallantry on the battlefield!

DOORS OF HONOR

As I was driving all alone, I began to think,
of the doors of honor I'd walked through in my life.
One to dense jungles, invisible enemy on every brink,
living life by each second, saturated by fear and strife.

I endured it all, though scorned by the nation I love,
plagued by wounds in body, haunted by dreams of horror.
Yet I loyally served with a strength from above.
On me they could depend, as I passed through this door.

While driving along, another door came to mind.
This one did open to a love beyond compare.
Always focused, I never chased rabbits of any kind,
but this "Lil' Rabbit" captured my heart unaware!

She e'er sang a "Melody" of lasting endearment.
The beauty of her tune filled my soul forever.
The softness of her being led to lifelong contentment.
An honor to love her through countless endeavor.

As I continued to drive, a final door grabbed my thought.
Wide open it was to the privilege of two boys.
I loyally assured them through every value I taught.
You can depend me, through both sorrows and joys.

Now they are grown, as my drive has come to an end,
healthy and strong, facing doors of their own.
May each one lead to honor, on which others can depend.
Let my own doors of honor guide you safely along.

COLLEGE FOOTBALL IS BIG deal here in East Tennessee! We love our University of Tennessee Volunteers! We do many celebrant services for those who were devoted to the "*Big Orange*", and the following poem serves to kick off each one of them. Obviously, not everyone in the country follows U. T. football (although they should), but feel free to manipulate the wording and colors to fit the football team of your choice.

COULD IT POSSIBLY BE?

Do you feel it? The warmth starts to flee!
Crisp air settles in and sharply chills me!
What does this tell me, could it possibly be?

No birds in flight 'tween the emerald trees,
only falling yellow-orange and burning red leaves!
What does this tell me, could it possibly be?

Cumberland Avenue, colored orange like a morning sea.
Above it, fogs of breath hovering anxiously.
What does this tell me, could it possibly be?

Parking lots smoke with sizzling delicacies!
Pop tops fly with the greatest of ease!
What does this tell me, could it possibly be?

Now I hear it, music smartly marching in beat!
Is the Pride of the Southland calling me?
What does this tell me? Could it possibly be?
Is it finally football in Knoxville, Tennessee?

WHEN READING THIS NEXT poem, it will not take you long to discover this man's favorite movie! Using the *Casablanca* theme, I was able to develop a poetic tribute to the loving relationship he had with his wife.

A CASABLANCA ROMANCE

"Of all the joints, in all the towns, in all the world,
she walked into mine!"
It may have been dark, it may have been late!
'Twas not important! "We had a date with fate!"

Romantic melody grew from the start,
music of love with my darlin' "shweetheart!"
A song that made me who I truly am,
May it never end! "Play it again! Play it, Sam!"

Tough times and demons may have got in the way,
but we ne'er let go at the end of the day.
For we knew for sure, e'en when filled with worry,
"It's all the same old story—a fight for love and glory!"

"Kiss me! Kiss me, as if it were the last time",
until we meet again in a realm sublime!
I'll be waitin', though adieu I now must bid,
to sweetly remind you, "Here's lookin' at you, kid!"

UNFORTUNATELY, WE FACE FAMILIES of loved ones who have greatly suffered for a long time prior to their death. Thus it was for this courageous lady, who dulled the pain with love for her family and the little things in life that thrilled her.

THE LOVES OF MY LIFE

Oh the things I loved so dear while traveling
through this life!
Things that caught my fancy, though they
often were quite old.
Whether ancient dolls or antique plates
that shimmered in the light.
To me they were my fortune,
as though 'twere bags of gold!

Yea my heart contained a love for music,
but not of modern times!
I'd rather fill my head with sounds
of classic country and rock!
A jukebox offering Elvis, Loretta or Cher
is where I'd drop my dimes!
For they brought me peace and joy,
as the pain they oft did block!

But the things of life we cherish and love
can't follow at life's end!
'Tis impossible to take as we slip
through that mysterious curtain!
The only one that can tag along is love
for family and friend.
Eternal it is for all of you!
Feel it, fore'er my love is certain!

YET ANOTHER CELEBRANT SERVICE for a lady who also loved to cook! She was quite talented in making her cuisines, but never really took advantage of cookbooks to make her scrumptious masterpieces. With just a little pinch of this, and a little pinch of that, she somehow made it all work. A fact I took advantage of in poetically revealing her way of approaching life.

A RECIPE FROM ABOVE

Lord, how do I make a life filled with love?
What is the recipe You've written from above?
A little of flowers? A pinch of care?
Maybe a smidgeon of just being fair!

Lord, how do I make a life serving others?
What is the recipe for helping sisters and brothers?
A little of sacrifice? A pinch of teaching?
Maybe a smidgeon of my hand just reaching!

Lord, how do I make a life close to You?
What is the recipe to daily walk as You do?
A little of prayer? A pinch of grace?
Maybe a smidgeon of Scripture embrace!

Lord, how do I make a worry free life?
What is the recipe to overcome the strife?
A little of faith? A pinch of can do?
Maybe a smidgeon of just walking with You!

WHAT A TRIBUTE TO be remembered as a person of honor! This poem describes such a man! One who spent his entire life living every moment with the goal of showing honor in all that he did and everything he experienced.

A MAN OF HONOR

Valiant and brave or wise, if you choose,
the meaning of my name, and that's not a ruse!
Did I fit this role, while through life I did wander?
I'd rather be remembered as a Man of Honor!

Oh, I pulled some pranks, funny things I would do,
like hiding in wait to scare Nanki Poo!
Yet live by my word with an ethical soul,
to be a Man of Honor was my ultimate goal!

I lived at my pace, oft responding to your decry,
"I'll get to that later! All I have to do is die!"
For life is too short to fill with busy to do.
A Man of Honor fills it with joy and what is true!

I loved the outdoors, in awe of God's nature!
My sanctuary for worship was shared by His creatures!
For in this masterpiece He paints His glory and grace,
where a Man of Honor is sure to see His face!

Some men seek fortune, some lust for fame.
Some will be selfish and cheat through life's game!
Is that a legacy that endures once they part?
Nay! But a Man of Honor will e'er live in your heart.

I WROTE THE FOLLOWING poem for one of the most difficult celebrant services I have ever had to lead. This one for a young man, age forty, who was found deceased by his mother, with no explanation as to why he passed. She had devotedly taken care of him due to the disabilities he received from a motorcycle accident twenty years prior. Obviously, this was devastating for her and the man's 13-year old son. What was so crushing for this mother, however, was that her other son had passed away under similar unanswered circumstances, five weeks earlier! He was only *thirty* years old! This poem was an effort to help her deal with the question of "*Why?*" Composed as though written by her eldest, it attempts to deliver reassuring comfort and hope from both him and his brother.

OUR PROMISE

We never had the chance to properly say goodbye.
We're sure you're plagued with anguish as to the question "Why?"
Though now we know the answer, we can't share across the divide.
Just rest assured we wait for you, on the glorious other side.

'Tis impossible to know the length of one's lifespan.
'Twas preordained long ago, as part of God's wise plan.
Our time we spent with you seemed unnecessarily brief.
But our purpose now is for His glory. Let that gently ease your grief.

Alas! I'm finally able again to wrap my protective arms,
around my little brother, to shield him from all harm.
Not needed though, for in this land that stretches far above,
there are no threats of danger, only perfect unlimited love.

Emptiness we know must haunt you, while days slowly pass by.
We, too, long to be with you to hold you when you cry.
But trust in the two wonders that will never ever depart.
Our love for you and His Amazing Grace, will always be in your
heart.

SOMETIMES WE CAN PICK up even the simplest things that families give us in describing a loved one filled with passion. In this case, these children's mother loved the color blue. I took that characteristic and used it to accentuate the truth that although she had many loves in life, her greatest love was for her family and friends! Even when she devotedly served the needs of her patients, as a skilled nurse.

THROUGH EYES THAT LOVED THE COLOR BLUE

Though brilliant and headstrong, stressing the point in rational way,
let me offer this point as you remember me today.
As I looked through eyes that loved the color blue,
I never stopped passionately loving you.

Though I delved in murder mysteries, as in my ear played classic rock,
let me assure you while time raced around the clock,
I read through eyes that loved the color blue.
And I never stopped passionately loving you!

Though I loved to travel and stroll in our mountains of wonder,
let me whisper to you softly as you sit and ponder.
As I gazed at the beauty 'neath the sky so blue,
I never stopped passionately loving you!

Though through long hours and nights I served my patients with skill,
let me speak with confidence while it's quiet and still.
As I carefully watched them through eyes that loved the color blue,
I never stopped passionately loving you!

Though I am gone and not physically on this earth,
let me depart with this message for all it's worth.
Remember how I saw life through eyes that loved the color blue.
And that I never stopped passionately loving you!

NATURALLY, MOST OF THE celebrant services I lead deal with a loved ones who have lived a long life–well into their eighties and nineties. This next poem is no exception; however, she always, even to the end, approached life with a young heart. In her mind, she was never older than twenty nine! With that, look at how this fun-loving woman faced life!

I WAS ONLY TWENTY NINE!

Remember the song by that band of lore?
"Will you still need me, when I'm sixty four?"
Well, I could never call that a dear song of mine,
for as you all know, I never passed twenty nine!

What a delight it was to stay young at heart,
with a laughter and love that would dare not part!
I was filled with pranks and oft' teased your spine!
What else could you expect? I was only twenty nine!

If I may say, I was a lady of "class",
with a champagne taste, but a beer pocket, alas!
Shopping was truly a passion of mine,
e'er prowling through "young misses",
since I was only twenty nine!

Forced to grow up fast, since the age of twelve,
I quickly became "The Boss", ensuring denial of self!
It was always about you, whom I loved without decline.
I never became weary, for I was only twenty nine!

ALL OF US IN the funeral business, dread those times when we must serve the families who have lost a baby or small child. Nothing tugs at our heart strings more than this crushing experience endured by our families. This child only lived three days! May this following poem help you in serving these families, with loving compassion for their grief.

MY SPIRIT NEEDED TO FLY

As much as I fought to stay with you,
I had to say goodbye.
'Twas not my choice to leave you,
but my spirit needed to fly.

For months you gave me warmth and safety,
as you nourished me within your womb.
I was an active part of you,
you and I oft sang the same tune.

Three days I cuddled in your gentle arms,
feeling beats of your loving heart.
I listened to your whispers of love,
until the day we had to part.

But one thing is for certain and sure,
though I no longer live on your earth.
You'll always know I'm cuddled in your heart,
softly whispering, "Thank you for my birth!"

THERE ARE ALWAYS THOSE in life who just know how to fix things! My father is a man like this! Such was this man, who not only was always available to repair the broken possessions we need in our own lives, but was also gifted in fixing broken lives and relationships with his gracious gift of forgiveness and understanding.

THE ULTIMATE FIXER UPPER

Long ago, before the shows raged on TV,
I was the go to for making it right.
Problems you say? Repairs you need?
Nothing was beyond my innovative might!

Whether painting or working wood,
or ensuring stoves got hot for supper,
All those I knew without doubt understood.
I was the first and ultimate fixer upper!

Life is too short to contend with things broken,
especially relations with one another!
Why hold grudges with the words unspoken,
words of forgiveness graced on your brother!

We all make mistakes, for we're human you see!
Sin in this world is a powerful corruptor!
But let us learn from error, let me help set you free!
For I specialize in being the ultimate fixer upper!

THE WOMAN, WHO IS the subject of this poem, loved Christmas! Her name was Myrna. She was also known as a living beacon of light that led many people in her life to the enriching and sustaining value of her love. She was always there for everybody, eager to brighten their day.

THE STAR WITNESS

Star of wonder, star of light,
star with loyal beauty bright!
Westward leading, e'er proceeding
guided us to the perfect light.

God created this star that shone.
For three score or more it gloriously glowed.
It led those who saw it with grace so mild,
to hope only found in the King Christ Child.

Wise men followed its glow all ablaze,
as it brought them to a Grace that simply amazed.
Foolish men did refuse with stubborn will.
But it lovingly continued to shine on them still.

Its name revealed the fine fuel of its toil,
'Twas "Myrrh"na, the valuable sweetest oil.
Soothingly, sweetly she revealed so bright,
The Way, The Truth, to The Eternal Life.

The star may be dark now, as it seemed to depart,
but its glowing oil can still sooth our hearts.
Its aura may have faded, but not end of story.
It forever glows brighter in the Christ Child's glory.

TAKE A MOMENT TO read about a grandmother who dearly loved her children. A love only matched by the love her children had for her! She even used the cookies she would bake to remind them to savor the blessings they have.

NANA'S COOKIES

Nana, our tummies desire something sweet!
Oh please can you tell us if you have such a treat!
Surely something exists in your cozy kitchen
that will scratch this nagging hunger itchin'!

Of course I do! Don't I always supply?
It's filled with cookies of sheer delight!
Just reach in and take whatever you might!

Oh savory cookies! Imagine the thrill!
Let us climb up a chair and grab our fill!
Two in each hand and one in the mouth!
We'll stuff our pockets 'til they all bulge out!

Now we'll open wide and take that first bite!
That sugary taste should be out of sight!
Yummy! No yucky! Our mouths pucker up!
Something's amiss! Something's corrupt!

Nana, what's wrong? These cookies are awful!
Why do they seem like a sugarless waffle?
It's a trick I learned in depression years past!
You see, the blander the cookies, the longer they last!

ON SEPTEMBER 16, 2007, my first wife lost her courageous battle with cancer, ending our thirty-four years of marriage. She did so, however, in glorious fashion.

About four weeks earlier, when she knew she was in trouble, she awoke in her hospital room with a keen sense of peace about her. She calmly looked over to me and said, *"Good morning. You know what I saw last night? An angel!"*

Of course, I asked her if she had been dreaming, and she replied, *"No! I was wide awake, and saw him standing at the foot of the bed! He said nothing, yet gave me the sweetest look."*

A few hours before she passed away, my daughter and I were in her room holding her hands. She labored with her breathing and could barely speak. Yet, somehow, she was able to turn to me and strongly proclaim, *"Trumpets! I hear trumpets! Don't you hear them?"* Five times she repeated this statement!

In both instances, she certainly gave living reality to those precious words from Scripture, *"I will never leave you, nor forsake you."* Through it all she taught me a valuable lesson, which is reflected in this next poem.

THE MOST IMPORTANT

I held her hand, as she struggled for dear life;
I thought of great moments I had spent with my wife.
Hundreds, maybe thousands, they were all in a swirl;
the special ones, however, began to unfurl.

Those romantic encounters sensually filling the air;
the soft kisses and embraces that removed every care.
Her holding my hand as we walked in the night;
on a bench, eating ice cream, watching sailboats in flight.

The excitement and fear as three children she gave birth;
yet the pain and the anguish bore riches of true worth.
The plays, the concerts, the games they would play,
we watched with great joy as we cherished each day.

Santorini sunsets, as we dined o'er the sea;
can't remember the meal, only her eyes watching me.
Viewing whales and otters from the coast of Carmel;
how her heart filled with bliss, it was easy to tell.

What was most important of all the precious times?
Of the moments in life, what towered in her mind?
Was it camping around a fire in crisp, night air?
Was it cruising the Caribbean, with time unaware?

Then in the darkness, her labored voice began to untangle,
as she whispered "I hear trumpets, the trumpets of angels!"
Five times she declared of that glorious sound,
as her Lord 'twas lifting her soul from earth's bound.

Then I realized the most important in her fifty-four years,
as I held on and kissed her through all of my tears.
She taught me a lesson, when her soul finally left;
most important is God's greeting, when you take your last
breath.

NOT ALL HAVE THE advantage of living a life of riches and valuable posses-
sions. Thus was the man I described in this poem. He was just a "*good ol'
country boy*", who lived a simple life, filled with football, NASCAR, cowboy
shows, country music and fast food delights! He never had much that we
would consider valuable. But there was one thing he proudly proclaimed,
and that was the riches he had in his children, grandchildren and great
grandchildren (*Little Boogers*).

A GOOD OL' COUNTRY BOY

Okay, so I like hot dogs and pizza,
banana puddin' and red velvet cake!
What else could be better eating for goodness sake?
These are a few things that brought my joy.
For I was born a good ol' country boy!

You know I loved my football and westerns and the thrill of a
NASCAR race.
They could easily put a big ol' smile on my face.
These are a few things that brought me joy.
For I was born a good ol' country boy!

Now my music was quite simple and resounded through my
bones.
But just the old favorites from the likes of Twitty, Waylon and
Jones!
These are a few things that brought me joy.
For I was a good ol' country boy!

But the loves of my life contained the strands of my DNA!
Kids and grandkids and little boogers made my day!
They were the main things that brought me true joy!
For they were the riches of a good ol' country boy!

CELEBRANTS OUT WEST SHOULD love this next poem. This woman and her husband ran a large cattle ranch in southern Florida for twenty five years! We don't have many cattle ranchers in east Tennessee, so this service was an exciting experience for me. If you can use this poem, and the deceased is a male, simply change it to *"cowboy"*! If the service is non-religious, just remove the last stanza.

THE LIFE OF A COWGIRL

Drivin' them doggies day after day!
Ropin' and brandin', rewarding with hay!
Ridin' the range to show them the way.
The life of a cowgirl! Yippee Ki Yay!

Watchin' them closely, making sure they don't sway.
Singin' so softly, to keep them at bay.
Tall in the saddle, while deer and antelope play!
The life of a cowgirl! Yippee Ki Yay!

Cowpokes get hungry, but they knew 'twas okay!
For I filled their guts, three times a day!
They loved my vittles, especially my filet!
The life of a cowgirl! Yippee Ki Yay!

Although it seems sunset, as before you I lay,
the trail never ends, my Savior does say!
His cattle on a thousand hills will ne'er go away!
Eternal life for a cowgirl! Yippee Ki Yay!

THIS LOVING GENTLEMAN WAS a giver! He was a generous blood donor all his life! He was also one who generously gave his time, love, understanding, and forgiveness to all he knew, especially to his family. Again, if your service is not religious, take out the last two stanzas, and change the second line of the poem to read: *Sixty five years it was allowed to flow.*

MY BLOOD

My blood provided a precious life for me.
Sixty five years God allowed it to flow.
It filled my cells with nutrition and strength,
and enabled my love to strive and glow.

I gave my blood, time and time again,
to enable others to recover and heal.
I kept the bank full for others of my type,
lovingly answering each fervent appeal.

I shared my blood to create two others.
Miraculous children that kept my heart
soaring.
Who through the red flow I never stopped loving.
Nothing could stop me from forgiving and
adoring.

Alas, as for all, my blood ceased to flow,
near to the biblical three score and ten.
Yet because of faith in the risen Lord's sacrifice,
my blood flows forever in His glorious Heaven.

So my final plea for all I love dear,
let your blood e'er flow with love for others.
Love God with heart, mind, soul and strength.
And prove you do by loving sisters and brothers.

THE FOLLOWING POEM WAS for a truly "*rags to riches*" guy! Raised in utter poverty and difficult home life, he pulled himself up from his boot straps with determination and grit! He eventually created an extremely successful ice company, along with a manufacturing company that made the ice containers one will find outside almost every store or gas station! Truly a man of determination and excellence, who instilled those same qualities into his sons!

STAND UP STRAIGHT!

What a journey I've walked while I was alive!
Those amazing years of four score and five.
Even failures would lead to success so great!
No matter what came, I could "Stand up straight!"

The poverty endured while raised in Texarkan',
shaped my mantra, "Get away from it as far as you can!"
Driving myself to break the bonds of this fate,
I freed myself, 'cause I could "Stand up straight!"

But the strength I needed to overcome the task,
came from the gift, in whose love I basked!
Sixty one years, she imaged God's grace so great!
It was her who helped me to "Stand up straight!"

So my sons, listen carefully to my advice!
Life is filled with challenge, at times as cold as ice!
Melt away the sorrows this world can oft' create.
Live with grace and purpose, and always "Stand up straight!"

OCCASIONALLY, WE COME ACROSS a celebrant service opportunity to serve the family of loved one who surpassed the century mark in years! The man this poem describes was 102! He outlived two previous wives! Up until the last three months of his life, he still drove his own car, was exceptionally articulate, was one of the best male voices in the church choir, and dressed impeccably wherever he went.

A TRIBUTE TO SHORTY

His name failed to match his many years here on earth;
long they were—one "O" two, from his birth!

Years filled with joy, filled with laughter, wit and grace;
the smile we always saw, seemed permanent on his face!

Snowy hair, softly flowing, gloriously crowning suits so fine!
His ques¬t—honor God with both appearance and mind!

A voice! What a voice! Songs echoed from his heart!
His role in the choir, one can ne'er fill his part!

Articulate, yet gentle, ever clear to the end;
O the wisdom he bestowed, how we long to hear again!

Only love, grace and faithfulness, his living lesson was so good!
Clearly he defined what it means to "walk with God!"

OVER AND OVER THE family of this loved one kept telling me how selfless she was. No matter what, even during her final struggles with disease and pain, she always kept a little mirror with her. Even while in the hospital, she would ensure the mirror was at her side to always make herself presentable in case a visitor might stop by. Simply delete the final stanza of this poem, if your service is secular.

IT WAS ALWAYS . . . ALWAYS ABOUT YOU

I can't say it was always easy during eighty two years of life.
There were times filled with wonder, yet moments filled with strife.
But even when burdens pressed me and I sought for what to do,
I trumped them all with love and laughter, for it was always . . . always about you.

At times it may have seemed as though I was a woman all strong and tough.
That I could withstand the pressures and strain, when others would say enough.
Like the delicate pansy beaming through snow 'neath skies all grey, not blue,
I displayed my petals of love and laughter, for it was always . . . always about you.

Yet my source of strength came not from self, for I was a human so weak.
I stayed upon the Scripture that with loving fortitude God did speak.
He so loved the world that He gave His Son to save me by grace so true.
And filled me with His love and laughter, saying, "It was always . . . always about you!"

THIS BEAUTIFUL LADY LOVED to read books—especially old Western novels! She was always known for read the *ending* of each book first, to see if it was worth reading! She also loved animals—*ALL animals*—especially her dogs and cats! Obviously, after you read the poem, you will also see had a special relationship with her dearest friend. A friend who greatly influenced her life.

GOD LOVES YOU, AND SO DO I

If I had first read the last page of my life,
I would've changed nothing, including the strife.
The end showed what drove that feisty twinkle in my eye.
Like Ms. Bedford said, "God loves you, and so do I!"

Chapters filled with critters I cared for and claimed.
All the raccoons, dogs and cats I knew them by name.
My ministry for God's creatures, came from on High.
Like Ms. Bedford said, "God loves you, and so do I!"

Paragraphs of prose formed my character in kind.
One never had doubt of what was on my mind.
Though we may have differed, separation was denied.
Like Ms. Bedford said, "God loves you, and so do I!"

But the overall theme threaded from beginning to end,
graced the pages of my years for family and friend.
For while Ms. Bedford and I gaze down from the sky,
that theme is what she said, "God loves you, and so do I!"

CAN YOU TELL ME what this guy's favorite movie was? It set the entire theme for the Celebrant service! Using that theme, this poem opens a conversation between he and his loved ones left behind (including his trusty Labrador *Rowdy Girl*), yet with a sense of warm assurance and hope! This is the service my wife, Kay, opened with an acapella performance of *Down to the River to Pray*!

BROTHER, WHERE ART THOU

O brother, where art thou? My siblings may ask.
I know I left suddenly, in fact quite fast.
Though alone, you may think, as that moment unfurled,
fear not, for by my side was trusty Rowdy Girl!

O brother, where art thou? You all may wonder.
Where could I be? Is it a place of splendor?
While you on that day did casually roam,
an angel band bore me away to my immortal home!

O brother, where art thou? Are you all alone there?
Many are here, and yes, my mother dear!
With a kiss and loving arms, she laid my head upon her breast!
And with joy I whispered softly, "I am weary, let me rest."

O brother, where art thou? Can you tell us we plea?
I'm with the One who cleansed and gave me victory.
Though on earth, my face you will see no more.
I plan to meet you on God's golden shore.

OH WHAT A REMARKABLE woman this was! She was 101 years old and had lived an adventurous and exciting life. She and her husband served together for many years in the Government USAID Agency, building roads in Laos, Thailand, and Yemen! This was during the 60s, when the political climates in these areas were quite dangerous and unsettled.

NOW FLY AWAY!

A feisty little bird for a century and one in all,
secured in God's nest, He ne'er let me fall.
Weathering the storms 'neath many skies grey!
Until He said, "It's time to go! Now fly away!"

I saw it all, from vinyl plastic to Bluetooth, too!
From horse and buggy, to planes beyond the blue.
Amazing technologies seemed to grow every day.
Until He said, "I can beat that! Now fly away!"

Hither and thither, I seemed to race through life's arena!
Was I the feisty subject of "Little Old Lady from Pasadena?"
Pedal to the metal, my foot was lead some did say!
Until He said, "You ain't seen fast! Now fly away!"

I gave my all to serve the most needful lands.
Building roads for travel through jungle and sand.
But God's wings protected through dangers at play.
Until He said, "You've done well! Now fly away!"

THIS NEXT POEM WAS about an electrical engineering genius! He worked for both the Zenith and Phillips/Magnavox companies for many years, where he was the owner of numerous patents. If it had not been for this gentleman, none of us would have ever enjoyed the beautiful sounds coming from the Allegro Stereo System, 8-track tapes, 4-track cassettes, and today's compact discs!

BEYOND THE ULTIMATE ZENITH

Reaching for tomorrow, my mind I kept fed.
All my life I was ever moving ahead.
Creative dreams, that some saw to be myth,
I ever pushed forward beyond the ultimate zenith.

Reaching for tomorrow, not for me, but all mankind.
I worked to enhance music yet to be refined.
To deliver sweet waves as a melodious gift,
I ever pushed forward beyond the ultimate zenith.

Reaching for tomorrow, to keep family ne'er deprived,
I diligenily endeavored to enrich their lives.
To ensure their welfare with a bountiful kiss,
I ever pushed forward beyond the ultimate zenith.

Reaching for tomorrow, is the challenge I leave.
Keep dreaming to create and always believe.
Make the world a symphonic rose filled with bliss,
And ever push forward beyond the ultimate zenith.

THIS WOMAN'S LIFE TRULY matched the kind of books she loved to read—
romance novels! A life of love and benevolence, full of color and dance,
along with a mama-bear dedication to take care of her children! Her life
was but a romantic dream dedicated to the service of others!

I ONLY DREAMED OF YOU

Life was but a dream, filled with ever vivacious delight!
No matter what the circumstance, everything was always right!
I danced and danced in all the days I happily glided through.
And amidst their vivid colors displayed, I only dreamed of you!

I never put myself up front, to ensure my needs came first.
Nay! I knelt on bended knee to stay your hunger and thirst.
I endeavored to keep you warm at night with afghans crocheted in hues.
Your comfort was ever on my mind, because I only dreamed of you!

Like a juicy Harlequin romance, yay even racy ones at times.
My life was written with loving hands, performing deeds sublime.
Even if I could have read the ending first, as I was always known to do!
I'd do it all over exactly the same, because I only dreamed of you!

And as my book has ended, and you place it on the shelf,
never forget my lessons lived, putting others above yourself.
And though I live with angels, somewhere beyond the blue,
I'll always be there in your heart, for I will always dream of you.

As a retired United States Navy Master Chief Petty Officer, any time I have the opportunity to serve the family of sailor is an honor and privilege. These next two poems are dear to my heart.

Ol' Joe was a retired U. S. Navy cook! This service was held at a Veterans Cemetery, and included full military honors. So the entire service centered on his military service. There are literally thousands of past/present Navy cooks, so you never know when the opportunity to celebrate such a life will come along. Just change the below name to the one applicable to you.

THE NAVY COOK

Ships at sea o'er the rolling waves,
protecting our freedom every hour, every day!
Grey beasts on the ready, every inch, every nook,
Would be dead in the water, void the Navy Cook!

Brave seaman of salt within flexible hulls,
each have their duties of the load to pull.
Machinist mates or gunners, where'er you look,
but their mission would fail, void the Navy Cook!

Three times a day the galleys are full!
Hungry sailors up to tables they do pull.
Scarfing down cuisines, like that stuff on a shingle,
'tis the Navy Cook making taste buds tingle!

Twenty years of recipes kept by Ol' Joe.
Like meatloaf for five hundred, when needed so.
Dedicate to serve, not one sailor e'er forsook!
Joe was their mainstay! He was their Navy Cook!

THIS GENTLEMEN WAS THE "*man's man*" when it came to being a sailor! Life at sea is tough many times, especially the long separation from family during deployments. One must often rely upon his or her faith to fill the loneliness that can plague the heart. God, however, can be found anywhere, at any time, whenever we need him the most—*even aboard ship*! Of course, you can always use this poem to celebrate the life of one who served as a Merchant Marine.

WHILE ON DECK AT SEA

Can God be found in all His creation?
In soft blankets of snow, or Fall leaves on a tree?
In the grandeur of mountains, or canyons so deep?
Can He be found, while on deck at sea?

Watch the sun as it sneaks o'er the horizon.
The surface is glassy and calm as can be.
Dolphins snorkel as they glide through the portrait.
The face of God, while on deck at sea!

Waves spraying foam from the edge of the bow.
Filling the air with a salt so savory.
Gracing the pallet with a spiritual spice.
The taste of God, while on deck at sea.

Neckerchiefs flap, gently blowing in the wind.
Breeze firm and brisk sailing ahead full speed.
Like a hand of assurance, stroking the face.
The touch of God, while on deck at sea.

The aura, the flavor, the feel of His presence.
The majesty of it all brings you to one knee.
A Sanctuary for sailors so far from their home.
Worshiping God, while on deck at sea!

THIS POEM PAINTS A beautiful picture of a ninety two year old lady who dedicated her life to missions, both locally and abroad, and to serving the needs of others struggling in life—especially children and senior adults. She was always ready to tell the story of Jesus! As you will see, she was also an avid golfer, maintaining a 10 handicap well into her seventies! Her favorite Scripture was contained in the Book of Ecclesiastes and the Book of Ruth. I tied all this together to reveal the truly remarkable purpose of her life.

THY PEOPLE ARE MY PEOPLE

Whether as a child, so innocent and young,
or mature in years, all worn and feeble,
I was always there as your servant hero.
Reassuring with love, thy people are my people!

No matter the color, the nation, the creed,
I stood for you tall, like a church's steeple.
To share with you all the story of Jesus,
I kept my pledge, thy people are my people.

T'was a time and a season throughout each step of life,
like golf, the links were all different, never simple.
With your par as my goal, I aimed you toward soft greens.
Keeping eye on the ball, thy people are my people.

I taught you the faith e'er needed in prayer,
while my hands laid on shoulders of the sick or cripple.
And to do for others, void of selfishness and bias.
Living my promise, thy people are my people.

And now that I've teed off on that eternal course,
Eternally serving my Lord, ever gleeful.
Who will carry my clubs of grace there on earth,
to drive the cause, thy people are my people?

VIRGINIA WAS THE NAME of this beautiful lady! A name which can mean *A Young Maiden*. She loved to travel and witness first-hand the wonders of this world, from Europe to China, and of course even close to home to take in the marvel of the East Tennessee mountains!

THIS MAIDEN

Near four score years she graced us in life.
Her passions and fortitude were e'er in view.
Whether in pleasures of wonder, or moments of strife,
this maiden taught us how to keep gray skies blue.

The beauty of our earth seemed to capture her heart.
From delicate flowers to the grandeurs of creation.
Her curiosity of cultures, their antiquities and art,
filled this maiden's soul with adventurous elation.

From the richness of Europe and the mysterious Far East.
From local flowing waters to the mountains we hold dear.
All sights were equal, ne'er one was the least!
And this maiden kept all their glory ever so near.

THEN THERE ARE CELEBRANT services that are *special*! Such was the case for this delightful, *special* man. He spent more than fifty years of his life in a home for those with special needs. He was enthralled with the cartoon character, SpongeBob, which immediately became the theme to his service! He watched it all the time and had memorized almost every notable quote by all the characters. It is amazing how these quotes defined the man! In honor for his passion, we filled the chapel with SpongeBob balloons, cakes, an underwater scene of SpongeBob's home, and his favorite foods! Even our Funeral Assistants wore SpongeBob costumes to gleefully greet all those who attended!

Time always seemed to matter to him, and he would often remind you of that by pointing to his wrist, saying, "*Tick tick tick! Time to go!*" I used all of this to allow him to poetically say "*goodbye*" to the many there who dearly loved him.

END IT WITH "AT NIGHT"

Everyone knows SpongeBob was very special to me.
That cuddly yellow square who lives beneath the sea.
So silly he could be, always smiling with delight!
'Cause everything he said, he ended with "at night"!

Joy and laughter filled me, every time he did appear!
Even when I was sad, or my eyes were filled with tears.
His quips of life and wisdom seemed to make me feel alright.
'Cause everything he said, he ended with "at night"!

How I wished I could've eaten at the underwater Krusty Krab!
It's Krabby Patty and sesame seed bun I always wanted to grab!
So I used McDonald's hamburgers to satisfy my plight!
To me they tasted scrumptious, especially eaten "at night"!

But all things must end, "tick tick tick" 'twas time for me to go.
SpongeBob asked Patrick "When I am gone, whatever will you do?"
"I'll wait for you to return" was his answer void of spite!
So say that often if you miss me, and always end it with "at night"!

TALK ABOUT SOMEONE FULL of love and life, yet with an in-your-face way of capturing your heart! No one could fit the bill better than a woman born and bred in New York City, with Italian and Irish blood running through her veins! The concrete jungle has a unique way of teaching grace in one's life, and there was no doubt she had it. If you have ever walked the busy sidewalks of 5th Avenue or Times Square, you quickly discovered that grace is a necessity! Without it, total chaos would prevail, and the city would stop!

NEW YORK GRACE

Yep! I'm a New Yorker full of spunk and opinion!
And if that ain't enough, try adding Italian!
It may seem as though I'm a little rough and gritty,
but ya gotta be tough to survive in that city!

Hustle and bustle is the name of the game.
If you're crowded on sidewalks, just try the train!
But it keeps us close, amongst those buildings so grey,
as we struggle to survive throughout the day!

Though the Big Apple can seem cold and in your face!
It's a concrete lesson teaching patience and grace.
If you can't yield a shoulder to let a stranger pass,
you're gonna regret it, and it's doubtful you'll last!

www.ingramcontent.com/pod-product-compliance
Lightning Source LLC
Chambersburg PA
CBHW071059090426
42737CB00013B/2390